THE NINE SONGS

The Nine Songs

A STUDY OF SHAMANISM IN ANCIENT CHINA

ARTHUR WALEY

CITY LIGHTS BOOKS

First published in 1955
© George Allen & Unwin Ltd.

First City Lights Edition 1973
© 1973 by City Lights Books

Library of Congress Catalog Card Number: 73-84228
ISBN: 0-87286-075-2

COVER: Artist unknown, Sung Dynasty (11th - 12th century) screen painting on silk. Peking Museum.

CITY LIGHTS BOOKS are published at the City Lights Bookstore, 261 Columbus Avenue, San Francisco, California 94133.

Editorial & Publishing Offices: 1562 Grant Avenue, San Francisco.

PREFACE

I have published this essay separately because it will, I think, be of interest chiefly to students of shamanism and similar aspects of religion. If printed in a sinological journal or in a volume of miscellaneous studies it would be likely to escape the notice of most of the readers for whom it is intended. But the Nine Songs are also well worth reading simply as poetry, and I have tried, within the limits of a literal translation, to make them sing as well as merely say.

I am deeply grateful to two friends, A. R. Davis of Cambridge and David Hawkes of Oxford, who have read this essay and made many useful suggestions. They must not of course be held in any way responsible for the views that I express.

CONTENTS

Chang Wu, Imaginary Portrait of Ch'üh Yüan, from the scroll illustrating his *Nine Songs*. C. C. Wang Collection, New York.

Introduction

In ancient China intermediaries used in the cult of Spirits were called *wu*.[1] They figure in old texts as experts in exorcism, prophecy, fortune-telling, rain-making and interpretation of dreams. Some *wu* danced, and they are sometimes defined as people who danced in order to bring down Spirits. But it is clear that dancing was not invariably a part of their technique, and the idea that they were by definition 'dancers' is perhaps partly due to a popular etymology which equated *wu*, 'spirit-intermediary' with *wu*, 'to dance.' They were also magic healers and in later times at any rate one of their methods of doctoring was to go, as Siberian shamans do,[2] to the underworld and find out how the Powers of Death could be propitiated.[3] Indeed the functions of Chinese *wu* were so like those of Siberian and Tunguz shamans that it is convenient (as has indeed been done by Far Eastern and European writers) to use shaman as a translation of *wu*.

Early references to shamans, though fairly frequent,[4] unfortunately tell us little or nothing about how they set to work. The Spirit talks to or through the shaman; but whether the shaman receives these divine communications when in a state of trance or whether some incorporeal part of him climbs to Heaven and there converses with the deity is not made clear. Nor are we told how one becomes a shaman. There is a second century B.C. story[5] of a woman upon whom a Spirit first descended when she was ill, and it appears that afterwards it was only during spells of illness that she shamanized. The *maladie initiatique* is of course a common stage in the career of shamans, magicians and saints in many parts of the world, and shamans used often to be described as neurotics by European writers. With this view of them it is interesting to contrast the following passage from a discourse on the relations between men and Spirits supposed to have been delivered about 500 B.C. The shaman, according to this text,[6] is a person upon whom a Bright Spirit has descended, attracted to him because he is 'particularly vigorous and lively, staunch in adherence to principle, reverent and just; so wise that in all matters

9

high and low he always takes the right side, so saintly (*shêng*) that he spreads around him a radiance that reaches far and wide . . . This is of course an idealized picture, perhaps intended to apply only to shamans of a Golden Age in the past, such as the famous shaman Hsien (Wu Hsien), a divinized shaman who became one of the principal gods in north-west China, and figures in the famous imprecation of the country of Ch'in against the country of Ch'u, in which the King of Ch'u is accused of 'showing no fear of God on High in his August Heaven, nor of that very illustrious Great Spirit, the shaman Hsien.'

But to return to the question of how one becomes a shaman. The frequent expression 'shaman family' (*wu chia*) seems to suggest that the profession was often hereditary. But in Ch'i (northern Shantung) such an expression would have had no meaning, for there every family was a shaman family: 'among the common people the eldest daughter is not allowed to marry. She is called the "shaman-child" (*wu-êrh*) and is in charge of the family's religious rites. This custom still (i.e. *c.* A.D. 80) prevails.'[7]

Spirits constantly appear to men in dreams or simply as daylight apparitions and communicate freely, without the aid of a shaman; and the conditions under which they required a shaman as a necessary intermediary are not at all clear. The most striking example of this is the story about the spirit (or ghost, if you will) of Prince Shên-shêng of Chin. In 655 B.C. the Duke of Chin murdered his son, Prince Shên-shêng. In 650, after some years of sordid scramble for the succession, a brother of Shên-shêng succeeded to the Dukedom. One of his first acts was to disinter Shên-shêng and re-bury him without the rites due to a former Heir-Apparent. Shortly afterwards Shên-shêng's spirit descended from Heaven and appeared to one of his former retainers. He announced that he had complained to God (*Ti*) about the new Duke's insulting conduct, and God had promised that to punish the Duke He would cause his country to be conquered by a neighbouring country to the west. The retainer pointed out that it would be fairer if the Duke were punished in some way that did not involve the whole land of Chin. 'That is true,' said the spirit. 'I will talk to God about it again.' The spirit then instructed his retainer to go in seven days' time to a certain place in south-western Shansi, where he would find a shaman waiting. The retainer kept the appointment and, speaking through the shaman's mouth, the Spirit now said that God had given fresh instructions: the Duke was to be punished; but the innocent were not to be involved.[8]

For even the most meagre description of a shamanistic séance we have to wait till the fourth century A.D. In the biography[9] of a certain Hsia T'ung there is an account of two shaman girls who practised in what is now Chehkiang, south of the Yangtze delta. 'They were of remarkable beauty, wore magnificent costumes and sang and danced well. They also had the power to become invisible. At nightfall, to the accompaniment of bells and drums, strings and flutes, they would slit their tongues with a knife, "swallow knives, spit fire from their mouths, fill the whole place with clouds till there was complete darkness," or produce flashes of dazzling light.' Hsia T'ung, who disapproved of shamans, having been tricked by his relatives into coming to a performance which a cousin was giving to propitiate the soul of one of his ancestors,[10] found the two girls 'already leaping and whirling in the courtyard. There were spirit conversations, ghostly laughter . . . exchange of wine-pledges turn and turn about.' Hsia T'ung was so much horrified by the spectacle that without waiting for the porter to open the gate he broke through the hedge and rushed back to his home. This account is probably not accurate in its details, for it is high-flown and allusive in style, and from 'swallow knives' to 'darkness' is a quotation from a second century A.D. description[11] of a music hall performance. From the fourth century onwards holy men, particularly strangers from India and Central Asia (and later particularly Sogdians and Persians),[12] were credited with fakiristic performances such as tongue-slitting and belly-ripping; but there is, I think, no evidence that such feats formed part of the traditional shaman-technique in China.

The prejudice against shamanism which is displayed in this story went hand in hand with the rise and spread of Confucianism. It was founded, I think, on the saying attributed in more than one place to Confucius that one should 'revere Spirits, but keep them at a distance.' When in 32–31 B.C. shamanistic performances at the Chinese Court were abolished, this saying was quoted[13] by the minister who sponsored the reform. Opponents of shamanism also had a theory that 'when a ruler is addicted to the use of shamans, cases of baleful haunting (*sui*) become more frequent.'[14]

After the establishment of Confucianism as a State religion in the first century B.C. the governing classes tended more and more to look down upon shamans, regarding them at the best as socially inferior—putting them indeed on the same low level as professional entertainers, musicians, craftsmen and other specialized technicians, who were not regarded as gentlemen (*chün-tzu*), or at the worst were looked upon as impostors who traded on the credulity of the masses. Perhaps the last person connected with shamanism to reach a high social position was the wife of the famous administrator Huang Pa.[15] When Huang was young he held a post in the police-patrol at Yang-hsia, about sixty miles south-west of Kaifeng in Honan. One day when he was going on his rounds he happened to have with him in his carriage a skilled phrenologist. The phrenologist suddenly pointed to a woman who was passing and said, 'Either the books on phrenology are all wrong, or that woman is destined to become rich and great.' Huang Pa questioned the woman and found that she was the daughter of a shaman family in a neighbouring village. Such was his confidence in the phrenologist that he at once married her and despite her humble origin kept her with him, though he rose from one high post to another. When, after her death, he became Prime Minister (in 55 B.C.) he had her disinterred from a provincial grave and re-buried in the aristocratic cemetery at Tu-ling, a few miles from the Capital.

I do not know when people belonging to a shaman family were first debarred from holding official posts. This was certainly so about A.D. 70, when Kao Fêng[16] avoided office by saying that he came of a *wu* family and was therefore disqualified for public service. There is a later example of this in one of the Judgments (No. 81) of Po Chü-i (A.D. 772–846): N. is summoned by the Governor of his district to serve on his Staff. He declines on the ground that he belongs to a family of shamans and is therefore debarred from holding office. The law-officers sue him for misrepresentation of status. Were they right? Judgment: 'In "defiling himself" by claiming to come of a shaman family N. was obviously only seeking to decline the appointment in a way that could not give offence. He had a perfect right to remain a private person if he wished to do so.'

But another story shows that many centuries later the hold of shamanism even on the official classes was still strong. Round about 1330 Yü Pan,[17] brother of the famous writer and statesman

Yü Chi, was Assessor at Hsiang-hsiang, about fifty miles south-west of Ch'ang-sha in Hunan. It was a fairly large town and in 1295 had been made the administrative centre of a district. There came to this place a shaman who was considered a great acquisition, as he constantly warned people beforehand that there was going to be a fire in such or such a place, with the result that the fires were quickly put out. A Spirit (*shên*), he said, came down and told him where the fires were going to break out. In this way he had a great reputation as a prophet and was treated with high consideration by all the notables of the place. After a time he announced that war and other disasters were approaching Hsiang-hsiang. Panic set in and many of the inhabitants fled. At this point one of the shaman's accomplices confessed that it was he who, on instructions from the shaman, had started the fires. The rumour about wars and disasters had been started in order to facilitate an onslaught on the town by bandits with whom the shaman was in league. The shaman was arrested and confessed, but none of the other officials of Hsiang-hsiang, from the highest downwards, dared to pronounce judgment against the holy man. Yü Pan protested that they could not leave matters like that; but his colleagues all said, 'If he is to be condemned, you must do it yourself.' Yü Pan then gave a verdict against the shaman and the other conspirators, whose names the shaman had revealed.

Some more stories about ancient Chinese shamans will be found below, in the 'commentaries' where I discuss individual deities and their history. All I have attempted to do here is to quote a few passages which may help to orientate the reader in his approach to the Nine Songs which are the subject of this essay. These songs are to be found in a collection of pieces called *Ch'u Tz'u,* a title which has generally been translated 'Elegies of Ch'u.' Ch'u was a kingdom which round about the middle of the fourth century B.C. comprised parts of what are now the provinces of Hunan, Hupeh, Anhwei, Honan, and Szechwan.* That is to say it included about a third of the then existing China. In these songs shamanism assumes a particular form not known, I think, in the classic shamanistic areas—Siberia, Manchuria, Central Asia. The shaman's relation with the Spirit is represented as a kind of love-affair.[18] One is, of course, vaguely reminded of temple

* For the steps by which Ch'u from being a southern country became predominantly an eastern one, see below, p. 59.

prostitutes in the Near East, and of devadasī and Krishna's relations with the adoring cow-girls in India; but these are only vague analogies.

It is clear at any rate that the relation between the shaman and the deity is a fleeting one, and perhaps the closest analogy to it may be found in the situation of the *hito-toki jorō* (single-time concubines) chosen as temporary consorts for the visiting god at the time of certain Shintō festivals in Japan. Some *miko* (shaman) songs in the twelfth century Japanese collection *Ryōjin Hisshō* show the god clearly as a lover. For example:

Kami naraba	If you are a god,
Yurara-sarara-to	With a swing and a swish
Ori-tamae!	Deign to come down.
Ikanaru kami ka	Would any god
Monohaji wo suru?	Be shy about such matters?

In the Nine Songs the typical form is this: first the shaman (a man if the deity is female, a girl if the deity is male) sees the Spirit descending and goes out to meet it, riding in an equipage sometimes drawn by strange or mythical creatures. In the next part of the song the shaman's meeting with the Spirit (a sort of mantic honeymoon) is over. The Spirit has proved fickle and the shaman wanders about love-lorn, waiting in vain for the lover's return. Between these two parts may have come the shaman's main ecstatic dance.

The songs contain a number of meaningless cries or exclamations, and at the cesura of each line is the exclamation *hsi* which may (but this again is only a very tentative suggestion) represent the panting of the shaman in trance, a sound very familiar to anyone who has attended mediumistic séances in Europe. Almost always it appears to be the shaman who is speaking in the songs. It may not always be he who does the actual singing; singers (*ch'ang*) are mentioned several times, and may sometimes have sung his (or her) words, just as the chorus sometimes sings the main dancer's words in Japanese Nō plays. One might expect the Spirit to speak through the shaman's mouth. The shaman, says a writer of the first century A.D., 'strikes the Dark Strings (probably a shaman name for some kind of zithern) and brings down the dead, who speak through his mouth.'[19] And there are numerous stories of divinities and dead men speaking through shamans. As

14

we shall see, lines 9–23 in Song VII make better sense if attributed to the Spirit, and the first six lines of Song VI could, despite some difficulties, also be taken in this way. Elsewhere it generally seems that it is the shaman who is speaking, or else the chorus; in the latter case, either for the shaman or in comment upon what is happening. I have assumed dialogue only when the context seemed imperatively to demand it. It is quite possible (and this, I know, would be the view of some scholars) that I have pushed this principle too far and that there is more dialogue than I have indicated.

To what sort of performances do the Songs belong? References to a hall (*t'ang*) seem to show that they were carried out near or perhaps inside a formal building, and as in Song II the Spirit halts at an Abode of Life (*Shou-kung*), a sort of chapel for the worship of spirits, attached to palaces, it seems that they took place at the Court of some great personage, possibly the King of Ch'u. I take them to have been a set of rites in honour of the principal deities of the land of Ch'u at a time when the territories already extended far beyond the original homeland in the basins of the Yangtze and Han rivers. There is no reason to suppose that the songs represent a complete libretto of the performances. There may very well have been prose dialogue (improvised or otherwise); for example, the shaman may during the 'mantic honeymoon' (this, I ought to point out, is my own descriptive phrase and not a Chinese term) have pleaded with the Spirit on behalf of the people of Ch'u, securing promises of good harvests, immunity from floods and diseases and so on. This part of the programme would have varied according to circumstances and so not have formed part of the fixed liturgy. There may also very well have been some 'properties.' For example, the Western Mountain (K'un-lun)* may have been represented by a raised platform of some kind, and Heaven by a pole with notches cut in it to make the Nine Regions of Heaven. These, however, are only speculations.

Appended to the Nine Songs are a Hymn to the Fallen[20] (to warriors fallen in battle), and also a sort of *envoi*, making eleven pieces in all. But these last two did not, I think, form part of the original series.

Apart from a few unfamiliar and presumably dialectical usages the Nine Songs are in standard Chinese, as used by the ruling

* See below, p. 47.

classes in the various States of ancient China. It is possible that some or all of them started life in dialect form. Or again some (and this would apply particularly to Songs III and IV which have their scene south of the Yangtze) may even have originally been in a non-Chinese language. The main difficulty in interpreting the songs lies in the fact that the subject of the sentence is so often left unexpressed. Add to this the absence of number, gender and tense, and you will readily agree that there is bound to be room for differences of interpretation. These difficulties are by no means confined to very early Chinese and have led to controversies about the meaning even of lines by standard poets, such as Tu Fu (A.D. 713–770). But it must not be supposed that, as regards intelligibility, the case of the songs ever comes anywhere near to being so parlous as that of, for example, the Zoroastrian *gāthās*, in which the meaning of at any rate more than half the lines is uncertain.[21]

The Nine Songs owe their preservation to the fact that like other early Chinese songs they were interpreted allegorically. The shaman becomes a virtuous minister who after having for a time enjoyed the favour of his prince is discarded by him. The best-known similar case outside China is of course the Song of Songs, which would never have found its way into both the Jewish and the Christian Bibles if it had not been allegorized to meet the needs of later times. It was in this allegorical sense that the Nine Songs were understood till well into the twentieth century, although it was recognized from the second century A.D. onwards that the moral interpretation was only a sort of ultimate meaning, and that taken in their literal sense they were *wu* (shaman) songs. They were first translated into a European language a hundred years ago by the Viennese scholar Pfizmaier,[22] and since then there have been several complete or partial translations; but I do not think that any of these are satisfactory. My aim here has been to translate and comment upon them in a way that would be useful to students of the history of religion and interesting to the general reader. But I have added a few notes intended chiefly for sinologues. Mere translation could not possibly make the songs intelligible, and I have found it best to follow each translation by a running commentary. About the authorship of the Songs (that is to say, about the identity of the person who gave them their present form) and about their relation to the other pieces in the 'Ch'u Elegies' I have deliberately said nothing. These are questions which will, I am sure, be one day discussed by two younger scholars who have for some time been studying them. As regards the time when these Songs were put into their present form, I should say that the traditional dating (fourth to third century B.C.) seems quite reasonable. But of course the prototypes on which they were founded may in some cases go back to a much earlier period. In the cults with which the Nine Songs deal an immensely important part was played by various kinds of sweet-smelling plants. Their names naturally constitute a great difficulty for the translator. There was of course in ancient times no systematic nomenclature based on structural differences. One name often covered plants which we should put in quite different categories, and the same name had different meanings in different places and at different times. This is true, of course, of all popular, traditional plant nomenclature. Friend, in his *Flowers and Flower-lore* (1884) tells us that in his day 'cowslip' in Devonshire often meant fox-glove, but that at Teignmouth people called buttercups 'cowslips.' In North Devon, he says, fox-gloves are called poppies! That is also the sort of situation we have to deal with when flowers are mentioned in old Chinese texts. One solution would be to leave the names untranslated; but that is only possible if one is making a scholastic crib. In a translation like mine that aims at giving as far as possible an impression of the literary quality of the original, one must try to use English words, even if they are only makeshifts. Take the case of *lan*. The term used to be translated 'orchid.' Then someone discovered that it was really thoroughwort (*eupatorium Chinense*) which has nothing to do with the orchid family. But *lan* is the name that modern Chinese botanists give to the orchidaceae; and I have stuck to orchid as a translation of *lan*. 'Thoroughwort' is awkward to handle metrically and is not a word that would convey anything to most readers. Actually *lan* in ancient times seems to have been applied to many different kinds of aromatic plant.

Names of stars confront the translator with the same difficulty. There was, at any rate till a period much later than that of the Songs, a fluctuating and loose nomenclature, except as regards a few well-known constellations. Moreover names that figure later as those of stars may originally only have denoted features in the mythological topography of Heaven, without being identified with actual stars.

(1) *Wu* and *hsi*. There is an assertion, generally of a lexicographical kind, in several Chinese texts that *wu* means a female shaman and that another word, *hsi*, should be used of male shamans. But in practice shamans were called *wu* irrespective of their sex.

(2) See M. Eliade, *Le Chamanisme*, p. 188. Shaman is a Tunguz word which became current in English owing to its appearance in a number of travel books translated, chiefly from German, from the end of the seventeenth century onwards.

(3) See Kanō Naoki, *Shinagaku Ronsō*, p. 25. Professor Kanō found, some fifty years ago, that in the region south of the Yangtze when anyone was seriously ill his relatives sent for a *wu* who, having been copiously supplied with food and drink, fell into a coma which lasted for many hours. On recovering consciousness the *wu* gave an account of her visit to the Underworld and told the relatives of the sick man what she had learnt there about the chances of the invalid's recovery—whether the Powers of Death were implacable or whether there was some rite that would appease them.

(4) The occurrence of the character *wu* in the Honan oraclebones seems fairly certain, but the sentences in which it occurs are of very uncertain interpretation.

(5) The illness of Shên-chün, see *Han Shu*, 25 A. 21 a.*

(6) *Kuo Yü*, Ch'u Yü, Part II.

(7) *Han Shu*, 28 B. 30 b.

(8) *Tso Chuan*, Hsi 10th year.

(9) *Chin Shu*, 94. 3.

(10) 'One of his ancestors.' Or perhaps simply 'his father.'

(11) Chang Hêng's '*fu* of the Western Capital,' *Wên Hsüan*, 2. 14.

(12) As for example in Stein 367 (Tun-huang MSS.).

(13) *Han Chi*, ch. 24. 4 b.

(14) *Kuan Tzu*, 3.

(15) Huang Pa; see *Han Shu*, 89. 4 *seq.*

(16) *Hou Han Shu*, 83. 15 a.

(17) *Yüan Shih*, 181. The Yü Pan episode happened during the Mongol dynasty. The Mongols were shamanists and Mongolian shamans were officially employed at Court. But it is improbable that any of the officials at Hsiang-hsiang were Mongols or that the dread of shamans shown in this story was due to Mongol influence.

* References are to the Po-na edition of the histories. The text used in translating the Songs was the *Ssu-pu Ts'ung-k'an* edition.

(18) The 'love-affair' aspect of the Songs was first emphasized by A. Conrady in lectures at Leipzig early in the twentieth century. See Bruno Schindler, *Das Priestertum im alten China*, p. 28. For Japanese analogies, see T. Nakayama, *Nihon Fujo Shi* (History of Female Shamans in Japan), 1931.

(19) *Lun Hêng*, 20.

(20) *Chinese Poems* (1946), p. 35.

(21) According to a recent computation only one part in seven of the *Gāthās* is intelligible. See I. Gershevitch in *Literatures of the East*, p. 58.

(22) August Pfizmaier: *Das Li-sao und die Neun Gesänge*. In Denkschriften der Phil. Hist. Classe der Kaiserl. Akad. d. Wissenschaften, Vienna, 1852. An extremely good piece of work, if one considers the time when it was made and the meagreness of the material to which Pfizmaier had access.

THE NINE SONGS

Song I

THE GREAT UNIQUE

(Monarch of the East)

1 On this lucky day, good in both its signs,*
Let us in reverence give pleasure to the Monarch on high.
I hold my long sword by its jade grasp;†
My girdle-gems tinkle with a *ch'iu-ch'iang*.
5 From the jewelled mat with its jade weights
Why not now take the perfumed spray?‡
Meats I offer, flavoured with basil, on strewn orchids laid;
I set out the cassia-wine and peppered drink.
Now the sticks are raised, the drums are struck,
10 To beats distanced and slow the chanters gently sing,
Then to the ranks of reed-organ and zither make loud reply.
The Spirit§ moves proudly in his splendid gear;
Sweetest scents with gusts of fragrance fill the hall.
The five notes‖ chime in thick array;
15 The Lord is pleased and happy, his heart is at rest.

* The two signs marking the place of the day in the cycle of sixty days.
† A sword from the 'land of Ch'u' with an inlet jade grasp can be seen at the British Museum.
‡ Held by the dancers.
§ i.e. the shaman.
‖ Of the pentatonic scale.

COMMENTARY

I take it that the deity in question is a supreme god, similar to
the Shang Ti, 'God on High,' of the *Book of Songs* and other
early Chinese literature. Under the name Great Unique (T'ai I)
he had a tremendous vogue during the second and first centuries
B.C. In or about 133 B.C.* a man from Po, a part of Honan that
had previously been included in the Ch'u kingdom (whence the
Nine Songs are supposed to come), prevailed on the Emperor Wu
of the Han dynasty to make the Imperial cult centre round this
deity. The Great Unique continued to hold this position for
several reigns, and his cult as chief god was only brought to an
end (along with many other religious innovations of Wu's reign)
in 32 B.C.† The commentators say that the Great Unique was
called Monarch of the East (Tung Huang) because he belonged
to the eastern part of Ch'u; if that is true his chief cult-centre was
probably in Anhwei. 'Great Unique' is also the name of a star,
but he no doubt existed as a deity first, just as Jupiter the god
existed (or so I suppose) before Jupiter the planet. His cult
as a star-spirit (not as a supreme deity) continued for many
centuries.

This initial song differs from most of the rest in that there is no
love-affair between the god and the shaman, and that offerings of
food are mentioned. I take the person with the long sword to be
the holder of the ceremony, and the Spirit who 'moves proudly'
to be the shaman. 'The Spirit (*ling*) means the shaman,' says the
early commentator Wang I (*c.* A.D. 120). 'The body is the shaman's, but the mind is the divinity's,' says Chu Hsi in A.D. 1199.
'Possession' is not mentioned or implied in any of the other songs;
but from the second century A.D. onwards (and perhaps earlier) it
was regarded in China as the typical form of shamanism, and it
also holds this position among the Tunguz. It seems to figure
little if at all in the shamanism of the Altai peoples and
Mongols.‡

---

* *Han Shu*, 25 A. 19 b.   † *Ibid.*, 25 B. 13 a.
‡ Shamanism has many different techniques and it seems to me a mistake
arbitrarily to label one or the other of them as 'true shamanism.'

No personal pronouns are expressed in the original; there is no 'I,' 'my,' 'us' or the like. In English one has to commit oneself, but must be taken as doing so tentatively, as I have already indicated above (p. 16).

Song II

THE LORD AMID THE CLOUDS

1   I have washed in brew of orchid, bathed in sweet scents,
Many-coloured are my garments; I am like a flower.
Now in long curves the Spirit has come down
In a blaze of brightness unending.
5   *Chien!** He is coming to rest at the Abode of Life;†
As a sun, as a moonbeam glows his light.
In dragon chariot and the vestment of a god‡
Hither and thither a little while he moves.

The Spirit in great majesty came down;
10   Now he soars up swiftly amid the clouds.
He looks down on the province of Chi§ and far beyond;
He traverses to the Four Seas; endless his flight.
Longing for that Lord I heave a deep sigh;
My heart is greatly troubled; I am very sad.

---

* For these meaningless exclamations, see above, p. 14.
† See above, p. 15.
‡ *Ti.*
§ Chi has two meanings (1) N.E. China, (2) Central China. Either would make sense here.

COMMENTARY

The general form is typical; but on a reduced scale. Between lines 8 and 9 one has to suppose the tender meeting of the shaman and deity, and perhaps also the central dance of the piece. The erotic element is reduced to a single love-lorn couplet at the end. The Lord Amid the Clouds was served* at the Chinese Court in the second century B.C. by *Chin wu* (shamans from what is now Shansi, in N.E. China). As we have seen (p. 13) part of Shansi was included in the kingdom of Ch'u.

I take the speaker throughout to be the shaman, presumably in this case a woman.

* *Han Shu,* 25 A. 14 b.

Song III

THE PRINCESS OF THE HSIANG

1 The Princess does not come, she bides her time.
Chien! she is waiting for someone on that big island.
I will deck myself in all my handsome finery
And set out to find her, riding in my cassia-boat.
5 May the Yüan and Hsiang* raise no waves,
May the waters of the Great River flow quietly!
I look towards that Princess, but she does not come;
Blowing her pan-pipes there, of whom is she thinking?

Driving her winged dragons she has gone to the North;
10 I turn my boat and make for Tung-t'ing.
My awning is of fig-creeper, bound with basil.
My paddles of sweet flag, my banners are of orchid.
I gaze towards the furthest shores of Ts'ên-yang;†
But athwart the Great River she lifts her godhead,
15 Lifts her godhead higher and ever higher;
Reluctant, her handmaids follow her; for my sake heave great sighs.
And my own tears flow aslant in an endless stream;
I long bitterly for my Lady and am in deep distress.
My oars of cassia-wood, my steering-plank of magnolia
20 Do but chip ice and pile up snow.‡
Can one pluck tree-creepers in the water?
Can one gather water-lilies from the boughs of a tree?
When hearts are not at one, the match-maker wearies;
Favour that was but scant is lightly severed.
25 These rocky shallows are hard to pass,
Those flying dragons sweep her far away.

---

* Rivers that flow into Tung-t'ing, the huge lake south of the Yangtze.
† Not identified with certainty.
‡ Lines 21 and 22 mean 'I am merely wasting time,' and I wonder whether chip ice,' etc., is not also metaphorical.

In our union was no faithfulness, only grief has lasted;
She did not keep her tryst; told me that she was not free.
In the morning I gallop my horses through the lowlands by
　　the River;
30　In the evening I stay my course at that northern shore.
The birds are settling on the roof-tops;
The waters circle under the hall.
I drop my ivory thumb-ring* into the River,
I cast down my girdle-stones on the shores of the Li;†
35　On a fragrant island I pluck the galingale,
Hoping for a chance to give it to her waiting-maids.
Though I know that the time can never come again,
For a while I loiter, pacing to and fro.

* Worn to protect the right thumb against the bow-string, see *Li Chi*, 12. 2.
† Another river that flows into Lake Tung-t'ing.

COMMENTARY

We meet with the Princess of the Hsiang (Hsiang-chün) in the story* of the First Emperor's† visit to the south in 219 B.C. When he reached the Hsiang Mountain, a precipitous island in Lake Tung-t'ing, near where the Hsiang flows into the lake and famous for its shrine of the Hsiang goddess, a storm rose. The Emperor asked who this 'Princess of Hsiang' was, and was told that she was the daughter of Yao and the wife of Shun,‡ and was buried there. He was very angry and to avenge himself on the goddess for impeding him by raising a storm he cut down all the trees in the island and had the ground marked with ochre, as though he were branding a criminal. But another and perhaps earlier tradition§ is that the ladies of the Hsiang were daughters of God in Heaven (*T'ien-ti chih nü*), and I suspect that this was how she was regarded when Songs III and IV were first made.‖

In this song there is only an unsuccessful pursuit of the beloved, with no love-meeting, though the last lines seem to indicate that there had been a successful tryst in the past. It is of some interest in connection with this song that in A.D. 143 the shaman Ts'ao Yü¶ was drowned when going out in a boat to 'meet' the Dancing Goddess (Po-sha-shên) at Shang-yü in Chehkiang. But I think that our shaman in this song is miming the role of someone going out in a boat, rather than actually doing so.

---

* *Shih Chi* 6. 18 b.
† The Emperor who built the Great Wall and united China.
‡ Yao and Shun were legendary rulers in the dim past.
§ *Shan Hai Ching*, 5. 12 a.
‖ 'The Princess of the Hsiang and the Lady of the Hsiang in the Nine Songs are two goddesses (*shên*) . . . they are Spirits (*ling*) co-existent with Heaven and Earth. How can it be said then that they were daughters of the Emperor Yao?', says the fourth century A.D. commentator on this passage of the *Shan Hai Ching* ('Classic of Hills and Seas').
¶ *Hou Han Shu*, 84. 15 b.

31

Song IV

THE LADY OF THE HSIANG

1   God's child has come down to the northern shore,
But her eyes gaze far away; it makes me sad.
Nao, nao blows the autumn wind,
Makes waves on Tung-t'ing, brings down the leaves from the
    trees.
5   Over the white nut-grass my eyes roam;
I made a tryst with this fair one at curtain-time.
Would a bird roost amid the duck-weed?
What would a fish-net be doing at the top of a tree?*
The Yüan has its angelica, the Li its orchids;
10 I long for this royal lady, but dare not speak.
All is blurred as I gaze into the distance;
I see only the waters swirling by.
Would an elk browse in the courtyard?
What would a dragon be doing on the bank of the stream?†
15 In the morning I gallop my horses in the lowlands by the
    river,
At nightfall I cross to the western bank.
Someone says that my lovely one has sent for me;
I will mount my chariot and let him bring me to her.
Now I am building a bride-room down under the water;
20 I am thatching it with a roof of lotus leaves,
Walls hung with sweet-flag, courtyard paved with murex;
I strew scented pepper-plant to dress my hall.
Beams of cassia, rafters of tree-orchid;
Door-lintels of magnolia, alcove of white angelica.

---

* With this couplet, compare lines 21 and 22 of Song III, and lines 13 and
14 of the present Song. The meaning in each case is: 'I am wasting my time by
hoping for the improbable.'
† Dragons belong down in the water.

25 Creepers knotted to make a bed-curtain,
Split basil plaited into a floor-spread
Weighted down with white jades.
The floor strewn with rock-orchid, that it may smell sweet.
Angelica laid on the lotus roofing
30 And twined with bast of asarum.
I have brought together a hundred plants to fill the court-
yard,
I have set up scents and perfumes at porch and gate.
But from the Nine Doubts* in a troupe to fetch her
Spirits are coming, many as the clouds.
35 I drop my sleeve into the River,
I cast down my thin dress on the shores of the Li,
On a flat island I pluck the galingale
Meaning to send it to her that is far away.
Though I know that the time will not so quickly come again
40 For a while I loiter, pacing to and fro.

* The Mountain of Nine Doubts (this is perhaps only a folk-etymology of
the name Chiu I) was where, according to some accounts, the legendary emperor
Shun was buried. If we accept the idea that the goddess is Shun's wife, then we
must regard the Spirits as sent by Shun to fetch her back. If on the other hand
we regard her as God's daughter, then the mountain only figures as a generalized
abode of spirits.

COMMENTARY

What strikes one at once in reading this song is that it appears to be to a large extent simply another version of Song III. The commentators explain the relationship of these songs by reference to the story that the legendary Emperor Yao had two daughters, both of whom he married to his successor, Shun. I cannot, however, help thinking that the Lady of the Hsiang (Hsiang Fu-jên) is merely another name for the Princess of the Hsiang (Hsiang Chün), and that the two hymns represent local variants of a hymn addressed to the same deity. It is, however, probable that the person who put together the Nine Songs took them as being addressed to the elder and younger sister respectively.

The correspondence between the two songs is even greater than appears in translation. Compare, for example, the couplet (lines 35 and 36) in Song IV:

> I drop my sleeve into the River;
> I cast down my thin dress on the shores of the Li,

with Song III (lines 33 and 34):

> I drop my ivory thumb-ring into the River;
> I cast down my girdle-stones on the shores of the Li.

Here (in Song IV) the character for 'sleeve' is almost certainly a corruption of the character for 'thumb-ring'; both have the same right-hand half. The commentators have realized that the two lines in Song IV are a difficulty. Wang I (c. A.D. 120), for example, explains them by saying that the poet, dissatisfied with his treatment at Court, has decided to leave China and live among the barbarians, 'who do not wear clothes'! The character for 'thin dress' is presumably also a corruption of some character meaning girdle-ornaments or the like, offered as a courtship-gift, just as in Song III. The description of the bridal chamber built for the goddess has, I think, many parallels outside China. Here is one from the Hymn of the Daughter of Light which occurs in the

apocryphal *Acts of Thomas*, a Christianized but partly gnostic
work of about the second century A.D.:

> Whose bridal chamber is full of light,
> Redolent of balsam and every fragrance,
> Giving out sweet perfume
> Of myrrh and crushed leaf;
> And within is strewn myrtle.
> There is the sweet breath of innumerable flowers,
> And the door-posts are decked with iris.

Song V

THE BIG LORD OF LIVES

1   The gates of Heaven are open wide;
Off I ride, borne on a dark cloud!
May the gusty winds be my vanguard,
May sharp showers sprinkle the dust!
5   The Lord wheels in his flight, he is coming down;
I will cross K'ung-sang* and attend upon you.
But all over the Nine Provinces† there are people in throngs;
Why think that his task‡ is among *us*?
High he flies, peacefully winging;
10 On pure air borne aloft he handles Yin and Yang.§
I and the Lord, solemn and reverent,
On our way to God cross over the Nine Hills.||
He trails his spirit-garment,
Dangles his girdle-gems.
15 One Yin for every Yang;
The crowd does not understand what we are doing.
I pluck the sparse-hemp's¶ lovely flower,
Meaning to send it to him from whom I am separated.
Age creeps on apace, all will soon be over;
20 Not to draw nearer is to drift further apart.
He has driven his dragon chariot, loudly rumbling;
High up he gallops into Heaven.

---

* K'ung-sang means 'hollow mulberry-tree.' Various heroes were born miraculously out of such a tree. Later the name was taken to be that of a mountain in the east.
† i.e. all over China.
‡ 'His task.' Literally, 'the long-life and short-life.' The god has come to regulate people's life-span.
§ The two basic principles that actuate the universe; too big a theme for a footnote!
|| The nine chief mountains of China; but sometimes explained as the name of a mountain in Ch'u.   ¶ Unidentified.

Binding cassia-branches a long while I stay;
Ch'iang! The more I think of him, the sadder I grow,
25 The sadder I grow; but what does sadness help?
If only it could be forever as this time it was!
But man's fate is fixed;
From meetings and partings none can ever escape.

COMMENTARY

The title, *Ta Ssu-ming*, means literally 'The Great Controller of Destinies' (or 'Lives'). *Ming* means a decree, particularly God's decrees, hence 'fate' in general, and in a narrower sense God's decrees about when people are to die; so that *ming* comes to mean 'length of life,' 'life.' As we find the Ssu-ming in this song deciding whether people are to be long-lived or short-lived it seems best to translate his name by 'Lord of Lives.' This song is followed by one about the Little Lord of Lives. The two songs are about the same length, so big and little cannot (as sometimes happens with Chinese song-titles) mean a long song and a short song, addressed to the same deity. The Lord of Lives, like the Great Unique, was identified with a star, or with two or more stars, and it was suggested that the Big Lord corresponded to one star and the Little to another. But in Chinese tradition in general there is only one Lord of Lives, a very well known and often mentioned deity. I am therefore inclined to think that Song V was used at the main ceremony in his honour and Song VI at a lesser festival; hence the 'Big' and 'Little' in the titles.

At the Han Court in the second century B.C. the Lord of Lives was served by shamans from Ch'u,* and he was one of the familiar spirits of the woman who shamanized when ill.† He was credited with limited powers of healing: 'when an illness is in the marrow of the bones not even the Lord of Lives can cure it.'‡ A book§ belonging to the end of the second century A.D. says: 'Today . . . people carve a wooden human figure (of the Lord of Lives) one foot two inches high which, when away from home, they carry in a box, and at home keep in a special small shrine. They regard this deity as on the same level of importance as Heaven and Earth. This cult is very prevalent at Ju-nan‖ and other neighbouring districts. Offerings of dried meat are always made to him, generally in spring and autumn.' The author of the book was a Ju-nan man and is describing the cult as he knew it in his home

---

* *Han Shu*, 25 A. 14 b. The *Shih Chi*, 28. 17 b. mentions shamans from Chin (Shansi).　　　　　　　　　　　　　　　† See above, p. 9.

‡ *Shih Chi*, 105. 7 a.　　　　　　　　§ *Fêng Su T'ung*, 8. end.

‖ In S.W. Honan, within Ch'u territory.

39

country. He does not, of course, imply that the worship of the Lord of Lives was confined to Honan. It seems indeed also to have existed in early times in Ch'i (northern Shantung), for a bronze inscription* dating apparently from the sixth century B.C. records an offering of two jade goblets and eight tripods 'to the Great Lord of Lives.' Later the Lord of Lives became a household god, 'living among men,' and was often identified with the stove-god.† But the Little Lord of Song VI is clearly thought of as a heavenly deity.

We are in the fortunate position of knowing exactly what the Lord of Lives looks like: 'he is eight feet [six English feet] high, has a small nose, carries his head flung back, has a heavy moustache, and is very lean.'‡

I take the outline of the song to be as follows: The gates of Heaven are open, which means that the god is about to leave Heaven and descend. The shaman, as usual, goes out to meet him. She remembers, however, that China is a large country and hardly dares hope that the god will descend in her direction.

The god is 'handling' Yin and Yang, the two primordial principles, corresponding to shade and sunshine, female and male, soul and body, and so on. That is to say, he is adjusting them—keeping them in due balance, which will ensure good health, good weather, good crops, and so forth. The shaman joins him and is permitted to help him in his task, which consists in making sure that there is 'one Yin for every Yang.' This phrase also occurs in the *Hsi Tz'u*, a work of about the third century B.C., where it is followed by the statement that this balance of elements is 'used every day by ordinary people without their knowing it,' which corresponds exactly to: 'the crowd does not understand what we are doing' (line 16 of the Big Lord of Lives).

In lines 17 to 28 the god has abandoned his devotee and she is left, as usual, in melancholy and desolation. 'Handling Yin and Yang' has sometimes been taken to mean love-making. I do not think that the text as it stands can be understood in this way, but this may very well have been the meaning of the passage in its original form.

---

* See Kuo Mo-jo, *Liang Chou Chin Wên Tz'u*, p. 254.
† See *Li Chi*, 23, and commentaries.
‡ From the *Ch'un Ch'iu Tso Chu Ch'i*, a work of about the first century A.D., quoted in the commentary on *Hou Han Shu*, 59, 26 b, Life of Chang Hêng.

Song VI

THE LITTLE LORD OF LIVES

1 The autumn orchid and the deer-fodder*
Grow thick under the hall,
From green leaves and white branches
Great gusts of scent assail me.
5 Among such people† there are sure to be lovely young ones;
You‡ have no need to be downcast and sad.
The autumn orchid is in its splendour;
Green its leaves, purple its stem.
The hall is full of lovely girls;
10 But suddenly it is me he eyes and me alone.

When he came in he said nothing, when he went out he said
    no word;
Riding on the whirlwind he carried a banner of cloud.
There is no sadness greater than that of a life-parting;§
No joy greater than that of making new friends.
15 In coat of lotus-leaf, belt of basil
Suddenly he came, and as swiftly went.
At nightfall he is to lodge in the precincts of God.
Lord, for whom are you waiting, on the fringe of the clouds?
I bathed with you in the Pool of Heaven,‖
20 I dried your hair for you in a sunny fold of the hill.
I look towards my fair one; but he does not come.
With the wind on my face despairing I chant aloud.

---

* A kind of parsley.
† i.e. the people attending the ceremony whose beauty is likely to match the fragrance of the plants. But the meaning of lines 5 and 6 is very uncertain.
‡ Addressing the god.
§ When the people concerned are still alive, but cannot meet.
‖ Where the sun bathes; also the name of a constellation. I omit two lines generally agreed to belong elsewhere.

41

Chariot-awning of peacock feathers, halcyon flags—
He mounts to the Nine Heavens,* wields the Broom-star.†
25 Lifts his long sword to succour young and old;
Yes, you alone are fit to deal out justice to the people.

* Usually thought of in ancient China as lateral, not superimposed.
† i.e. comet; used by deities to sweep away evil.

COMMENTARY

In Song V (the Big Lord) the season is not indicated. But in the present song (the Little Lord) line 7 fixes it as autumn. The shaman appears to be speaking throughout. The love-meeting takes place after line 10 ('me he eyes and me alone'). In the next line it is over and the god has departed. For both Songs, see E. Erkes, 'The God of Death in Ancient China,' *T'oung Pao*, XXXV, 1939.

Song VII

THE LORD OF THE EAST

1   There is a glow in the sky; soon he will be rising in the east.
Now on my balcony falls a ray from Fu-sang.*
I touch my horses and gently drive.
The night grows pale; now it is broad daylight.
5   He harnesses his dragon-shaft,† rides on his thunder-
     wheels,‡
He carries banners of cloud that twist and trail.
But he heaves a great sigh, and when he is about to rise
He cannot make up his mind; he looks back full of yearning.
'*Ch'iang!* Beauty§ and music are things to delight in!
10 He that looks lingers, and forgets to go on his way.
The zithern-strings are tightened; drum answers drum.
The bells are beaten till the bell-stand rocks.
Sound of flute, blowing of the reed-organ;
A clever and beautiful Spirit-guardian‖
15 Lightly fluttering on halcyon wings.
Verses chanted to fit the dance,
Singers who keep their pitch, instruments in strict measure;
The coming of many Spirits¶ covers the sun.
Coat of blue cloud, skirt of white rainbow,
20 I gather my reins and my chariot sweeps aloft.
I take up my long arrow and shoot at the Heavenly Wolf,**
Then draw toward me the Dipper†† and pour out for myself
     a drink of cassia‡‡
And bow in hand plunge into the abyss,
Am lost in mirk and darkness as I start on my journey to the
     East.

---

* The 'propped-up mulberry tree'; the place where the sun rises.
† Chariot with dragons carved on the shaft.
‡ The thunder-god is always shown manipulating wheel-like objects.
§ Of the singing-girls.   ‖ i.e. the shaman.   ¶ Attracted by the music.
** Name of a baleful star. For the Shooting, see commentary.
†† Name of four stars in Ursa Major.   ‡‡ To celebrate his victory.

COMMENTARY

In the second century B.C. shamans from Chin (Shansi) served the Lord of the East (Tung-chün) at the Chinese Court.* I cannot help thinking that, mythologically speaking, he is the same person as Eastern Brightness (Tung-ming), the North Korean culture-hero who at the age of seven made himself a bow and arrow, and hit everything he aimed at.† Tung-ming's father was God in Heaven (T'ien-ti) who visited his mother in the form of a ray of sunlight.‡ Fu-sang, the land of sunrise, was later identified with Japan.

The shaman, as usual, goes to welcome the god. The god catches sight of the worshippers and in lines 9 to 18 describes what he hears and sees. Musicians are playing, singers are chanting and there is a 'clever and handsome shaman'—a tribute that the shaman pays to himself, the god's speech being, as I take it, spoken through the shaman's mouth. In lines 19 to the end the god's description of his own actions continues. He soars up again to Heaven, shoots the baleful Wolf Star, then using the Dipper Star as a ladle refreshes himself with a drink of cassia-juice. Finally, bow in hand (I doubt whether the Bow and Arrow constellation is here thought of), plunges into the abyss, to make his subterranean return-journey to the land of sunrise. There is no love-meeting or tearful parting in this song. As lines 20 to 23 in their existing order do not make sense I have assumed a confusion in the text. Line 20 becomes my line 21, line 21 becomes my line 23, line 23 becomes my line 20.§

---

* *Han Shu*, 25 A. 14 b.
† See *Hou Han Shu*, 85. 4 b, and *Wei Chih*, 30, 12 b (commentary).
‡ *Ch'ao-hsien Shih Luo*, I. 4 a. For the development of the Tung-ming legend, see R. Imanishi, *Chōsen Koshi no Kenkyū* (1938), p. 475 *seq*.
§ There is a translation of this Song by Maspero in *Journal Asiatique*, 1924, pp. 21–23.

Song VIII

THE RIVER GOD

(Ho-po)

1 With you I wandered down the Nine Rivers;*
   A whirlwind rose and the waters barred us with their waves.
   We rode in a water-chariot with awning of lotus-leaf
   Drawn by two dragons, with griffins to pull at the sides.
5 I climb K'un-lun† and look in all directions;
   My heart rises all a-flutter, I am agitated and distraught.
   Dusk is coming, but I am too sad to think of return.
   Of the far shore only are my thoughts; I lie awake and yearn.

   In his fish-scale house, dragon-scale hall,
10 Portico of purple-shell, in his red palace,
   What is the Spirit doing, down in the water?
   Riding a white turtle, followed by stripy fish
   With you I wandered in the islands of the River.
   The ice is on the move; soon the floods will be down.
15 You salute me with raised‡ hands, then go towards the East.
   I go with my lovely one as far as the southern shore.
   The waves surge on surge come to meet him,
   Fishes shoal after shoal escort me on my homeward way.

* The 'Nine Rivers,' constituting the delta of the Yellow River, belong to mythical geography.
† Mythical mountain where the Yellow River was supposed to rise. Later the name was applied to various real mountain ranges in the west. See above, p. 15.
‡ Hands folded in the sleeves and raised.

47

COMMENTARY

Of the deities that figure in the Nine Songs the god of the Yellow River is the only one who continued to be prominent in Chinese legend and whose cult went on till modern times. In Song VIII he is called Ho-po, which is his commonest name. This means River Elder. He is also often called Ho-shên (Spirit of the River), or simply Ho, 'The River.' He was a greedy god, often taking a fancy to and abducting mortal men's daughters, to add to his harem, or carrying off their sons to marry to his daughters, who figure largely in Chinese legend. Sometimes he merely took a fancy to people's clothes. Before a great battle (630 B.C.) in which the people of Ch'u were defeated by their northern neighbours, the people of Chin, the Ch'u minister Tzu-yü dreamt that the River God (*Ho-shên*) came and said (pointing to Tzu-yü's very smart cap, with cap-strings of threaded jade) 'give me that cap, and you shall have the elks of Mêng-ch'u,' meaning that Ch'u would conquer this district in Honan. Tzu-yü ignored the demand and in consequence the army of Ch'u suffered a great defeat.*

The god was at first simply the god of the Yellow River (and presumably of its tributaries), with a cult carried on by local people. But later he claimed the right to offerings of propitiation from all and sundry. About 490 B.C.† the King of Ch'u fell ill. The diviners said his illness was due to a 'possession' by the River and that he would not recover unless he sacrificed to the River. The king protested that rulers only sacrificed to rivers in their own territory. 'The Yangtze, the Han, the Sui and the Chang‡ are the rivers of Ch'u. They alone can affect our fortunes. My conduct has not been perfect; but against the Yellow River I have never committed any offence.' However, it paid to stand up to the god. A certain Han Ho-tzu,§ coming from the north, was about to cross the Yellow River when the boatman reminded him that everyone who crossed the River had to make an offering to

* *Tso Chuan*, Duke Hsi, 28th year.
† See *Tso Chuan*, Duke Ai, 6th year, and *Shih Chi*, 40, 21 a.
‡ The Han is in Hupeh, flowing into the Yangtze at Hankow. The Sui and Chang are in Honan. § See *Shuo Yüan*, 19.

48

the River God. Han Ho-tzu refused, on the ground that only the Emperor sacrificed to spirits wherever they might be; a stranger like himself had no obligation towards local deities. The boatman reluctantly put out from shore, but in mid-stream the boat began to turn round and round. The boatman said: 'There is no time to lose. We had better adjust our clothes and make ready to swim.' But Han Ho-tzu said he would rather die than pander to claims that were illegitimate. Whereupon the boat stopped revolving and safely reached the other shore.

I have said that the River God had to be appeased by giving him 'wives.' We read that at Yeh, in the extreme north of Honan, it was the custom* *c.* 400 B.C. to give the god a wife every year. The shamans went round from house to house looking for a particularly pretty girl. When they found her they gave her a good bath, dressed her in the finest silks and housed her in a special 'house of purification' on the river bank, where she lived in seclusion behind red curtains. After ten days or more they powdered her face and decked her out as a bride and set her afloat on a thing shaped like a bridal bed. After drifting some 10 *li* (five or six miles) down stream the bridal-raft sank and disappeared. 'People with handsome daughters,' we are told, 'fearing that the shaman would take them to "marry" to the River God, used to flee with their daughters to distant parts.' The place where the victims were launched was still shown in the sixth century A.D.† It was on the banks of the River Chang which now flows into the sea, but may then have been a tributary or sub-tributary of the Yellow River. Sometimes these sacrifices were made to appease the god when his waters were tampered with.‡ In 417 B.C. Duke Ling of Ch'in married a 'princess' (the god was given to understand that she was a princess, but in reality she was an ordinary commoner) to the god, when work was being done to deepen some rapids.

The River God figures in one of the finest passages of early Chinese literature—the Autumn Flood chapter of the Taoist work *Chuang Tzu* (third century B.C.?). In this apologue the River (the God's domain) is in flood. It is so wide that from one bank to the other one cannot distinguish a cow from a horse. In high glee the River God makes his way through glorious scenes of inundation

---

* *Shih Chi*, 126. 14 a.   † *Shui Ching Chu*, 10.

‡ *Shih Chi*, 15. 10 b.

till he comes to the sea. He looks eastward and can see no shore at all! In consternation he realizes that his own domain is nugatory compared with the limitless expanses of the great ocean.

In the second century B.C. there were 'River shamans' who served the River God not at Ch'ang-an, the capital, but at Lin-chin, on the west bank of the Yellow River, north of its junction with the Wei.*

Here is another story which shows that if stood up to manfully the River God is not always inexorable. About 30 B.C.† the governor of Tung-chün, in the S.W. corner of Hopeh, when there was a danger of the Yellow River breaking through an embankment, first threw a white horse into the river as a sacrifice, and then got a shaman to inform the god that the Governor intended, if the embankment was breached, to fill the gap with his own body. Soon, however, the embankment began to crumble. Everyone fled in terror except the Governor and one of his clerks who remained weeping by his side. Suddenly the waters began to recede, and the situation was saved.

In a story supposed to date from about A.D. 320,‡ a young man returning late at night to Hangchow meets a boy driving in a smart new carriage. The boy calls to him to come and get into the carriage, saying, 'My master wishes to see you.' The young man is then driven away into the darkness. Presently the road begins to be brilliantly lighted by long rows of torches, and they come to a great walled city. Above the main building there hangs a flag with the inscription 'Emblem of the River God.' The young man is taken in to see the god, who turns out to be very handsome, and does not look more than about thirty years old. The god tells him that he has a very studious and intelligent little daughter whom he intends the young man to marry. He does not dare to refuse, and a grand wedding ceremony is held, which lasts three days. The bride turns out to be a very attractive girl of about eighteen. On the fourth day the bridegroom is told that he will now be escorted back to the every-day world. His wife, parting with him tearfully, gives him a golden bowl and bag full of musk along with a large sum of money and three scrolls of medical recipes,

* *Shih Chi*, 28. 18 a.   † *Han Shu*, 76. 29 a.
‡ *Sou Shên Chi*, 4. 2 a. The story is probably later than 4th century; see *T'ai-p'ing Kuang Chi*, 295.
For the different versions of the *Sou Shên Chi*, see Toyoda Minoru, in *Tōhō Gakuhō* (Tōkyō), 1942.

telling him that he is to practise as a doctor for ten years and then come back to claim her. He has immense success as a doctor, but owing to his elder brother having died he feels he cannot leave his mother; and so, instead of claiming his spirit-bride, he marries a human wife and takes a job in the Civil Service.

We are not told that the River God exacted any punishment from him for failing to turn up after ten years. The god, indeed, had softened as the centuries went by and had also acquired a wider scope. He is no longer a local deity of the Yellow River; he has turned into a God of Waters in general. A ninth-century writer tells us how the god obtained timber for the building of his vast city. On the North River, he says, near Canton, there is a point at which timber being floated down from Hunan is invariably sucked down into the stream and lost.*

From another story† of about the same date we learn that dead men sometimes take service with the River God. A certain Wei P'u meets at an inn with a curious-looking individual who offers himself as a groom. Wei P'u is sorry for him and decides to give him a trial, but on their further journey strange and disquieting things happen. For example, an innkeeper's little son is playing near the gate. The groom walks up to him and prods his back with his fingers. The child is terrified and faints. The innkeeper sends at once for Miss Two, the best local shaman. To summon her familiar spirit, to whom she refers as 'Mr. Three,' the shaman plays on her *pipa*. Presently she stretches herself, sneezes, and announces that the spirit has come. She then has a conversation with the spirit, who tells her that the child is 'possessed' by a 'stranger-ghost.' The god describes the ghost, and the description is evidently that of the mysterious groom. The Spirit, speaking through the shaman, recommends that the child should be washed with a decoction of orchid (*lan*). This is duly done, and the child recovers. The groom then confesses that he is indeed a stranger-ghost (a displaced ghost, as we might say). Previously, he says, he was in the service of the River God, but they fell out, and now he is desperately searching for some fresh emplacement. Like other river-deities (for example the 'lord of Yang,' from whom the Yangtze is supposed to have taken its name) the god of the Yellow River is often supposed to have been a man who was drowned

* *Yu-yang Tsa Tsu*, Continuation, 10. 2 a.
† *T'ai-p'ing Kuang Chi*, 341.

51

and subsequently deified. The name he bore when a human being is generally said to have been Fêng I.

The amount of space I have devoted to the River God may seem disproportionate. The disproportion is due to the fact that among the deities who figure in the Nine Songs he is the only one about whom much is known. The others quickly fade out of Chinese cult and legend, and what I have said about them is, I think, all that is known. As regards the interpretation of the Song itself, no tense is expressed in the opening lines. But as I interpret it, the Song begins after the meeting is temporarily over; certainly after line 5 ('I climb Mount K'un-lun'), the shaman (presumably a girl) has already been deserted by the god. But it seems that at the end of the Song the god, before setting out for the East (now that the ice has melted), comes back to say good-bye to the shaman. Clearly other interpretations are possible.

Song IX

THE MOUNTAIN SPIRIT

(Shan-kuei)

1 It seems there is someone over there, in that fold of the hill,
Clad in creepers, with a belt of mistletoe.
He is gazing at me, his lips parted in a smile;
'Have you taken a fancy to me? Do I please you with my
lovely ways?'
5 Driving red leopards, followed by stripy civets,
Chariot of magnolia, banners of cassia,
Clad in stone-orchid, with belt of asarum,
I go gathering sweet herbs to give to the one I love.
I live in a dark bamboo grove, where I never see the sky;
10 The way was perilous and hard; that is why I am late for the
tryst.

High on the top of the hill I stand all alone;
Below me the clouds sweep past in droves.
All is murk and gloom. *Ch'iang!* Darkness by day!
The east wind blows gust on gust, spreading magic* rain.
15 Waiting for the Divine One I linger and forget to go back.
The year is drawing to its close; who will now beflower me?
I pluck the Thrice-blossoming† amid the hills,
Among a welter of rocks and vine-creeper spreading between.
Wronged by my Lord I am too sad to think of going back.
20 You love me, I know it; nothing can come between us.‡
He of the hills is fragrant with the scent of galingale,
He drinks from a spring amid the rocks,
He shelters under cypress and pine.

---

   * *Ling*; i.e. sent by Spirits.   † Unidentified.
   ‡ 'Nothing can come between us' is only a guess. The meaning is very
uncertain. It seems very likely that the lines in this Song have got into the
wrong order; but I have not ventured on a rearrangement.

You love me, I know it; despite all doubts that rise.
25 His chariot thunders, the air is dark with rain,
The monkeys twitter; again they cry all night.
The wind soughs and soughs, the trees rustle;
My love of my Lord has brought me only sorrow.

COMMENTARY

Mountain spirits (called *shan-kuei, shan-shên* or *shan-chün*, the last meaning 'Lord of the Mountain') played in ancient China a role parallel to that of River Spirits. In the second century B.C. a number of mountain spirits were worshipped. The only one whose territory lay in the previous domains of Ch'u was the T'ien-chu (Heavenly Pillar), the highest point in the Ch'ien-shan range in Anhwei.* The Spirit of Song IX may very well be the god of the Heavenly Pillar Mountain. Like river-spirits, mountain-spirits too demand human husbands and wives. When in A.D. 56 a certain Sung Chün was Governor of part of Anhwei he found that at a place near Lüchow the shamans were in the habit of taking boys and girls and dedicating them as husbands and wives of two neighbouring hills, the T'ang-shan and the Hou-shan, the latter meaning 'Queen Hill.' The boys and girls chosen were compelled to remain permanently celibate. Sung Chün put a stop to this by ordering that in future the spirits' husbands and wives were to be taken exclusively from the families of shamans. Whereupon the practice† ceased.

I take it that the person driving white leopards in line 5 is the shaman who, if the god is masculine, is presumably a girl. It will then also be the shaman who says 'I live in a dark bamboo grove.' Possibly the 'bamboo-grove' refers to some kind of covered bamboo construction (similar to the booths used by strolling players in later times) in which the shaman operated.

It would not be altogether impossible to take the divinity as a woman and the shaman as a male. It might indeed be thought that the opening suggests this. But though *jên* (man) can sometimes mean 'person' of either sex, the phrase *shan chung jên* 'man among the mountains' ('He of the hills' in my translation, line 21) would, it seems to me, be an odd way of referring to a female. But I may be wrong about this, and if it were possible in English to be non-committal about genders, I would have left the question open in my translation.

After Song IX follows, as I have said above, the beautiful

* *Han Shu*, 25. B. 2 a.   † *Hou Han Shu*, 41. 21 a.

55

Hymn to the Fallen which I have translated before (*Chinese Poems*, 1946, p. 35) and will not repeat here. There is also a short finale in five lines, apparently intended to be sung at the end of the whole ceremony:

> Now to the measure of the drums we have finished our rites,
> From dancer to dancer the flower-spray has been handed,
> Lovely ladies have sung their slow measures.
> In spring, the orchid, in autumn the chrysanthemum;
> So shall it be forever, without break.

ADDITIONAL NOTES

Song I. It is interesting to compare this song with No. 1 of the nineteen Han sacrificial hymns, *Han Shu*, 22. 16 b.

Song III, line 11.   *Po*, 'to strike,' should (as Tai Chên points out in his *Ch'ü Yüan Fu Chu*, Yin I, p. 5) be written 'bamboo' over 'water' *plus* 'white,' and means an awning made of wood-splints.

Song IV, line 26.   The meaning of *mien* is uncertain; something to do with the floor rather than 'rafters' seems to be required by the sense.

Song V, line 6.   There is no evidence for a mountain called K'ung-sang in Ch'u. The 'hollow mulberry-tree' in *The Great Summons*, coming as it does in the middle of a description of music, certainly means 'the zithern,' as has generally been supposed.

Song V, line 8.   Compare the reply of the diviner Ling-fên in the *Li Sao*: 'The Nine Provinces are wide and great; it is not only here (i.e. in Ch'u) that there are girls.' I am, however, far from being certain that my translation is right. The normal meaning of *ho tsai yü* would be 'How is it my (or 'our') business?' The early commentator puts these words into the mouth of the god and explains that how long we live depends on Heaven, who will give us long life or short according to our good or bad behaviour. But in that case the emphasis in line 7 on the vastness of China's population seems irrelevant. Moreover a moral idea is introduced of a kind that does not figure elsewhere in the Songs.

Song V, line 17.   The Han commentator says that 'sparse-hemp' (*su-ma*) means 'spirit-hemp' (*shên-ma*); but it is not known what 'spirit-hemp' is. *Su-ma* was evidently valued for its flowers, and there is no reason to suppose that there is any allusion here to the use of hemp as a narcotic or trance-inducer. There is perhaps a pun on *su* in the plant name and *su* meaning 'estranged,' 'apart' and so on. The name *ma* (hemp) was applied in ancient China to many plants that were not connected with hemp (*cannabis*) in our sense.

Song VII, line 12.   Text as restored by Wang Nien-sun in *Tu Shu Tsa Chih*, Yü Pien B. 5 b.

Song VII, lines 20 to 23.   Wang I specifically says that there are some displacements in the text of the Songs and this passage seems to me to be a clear case.

Song VIII, line 14.   The expression *liu-ssu* (flowing thaw) is usually written as here with the radical 'water' (not 'ice') in the second character. Compare *Hou Han Shu*, 20. 5 a, life of Wang Pa, 'an official came back and said: The river is "flowing and thawing" (*liu-ssu*); it cannot be crossed without boats.'

Song IX.   Both Wang I and the eighth century 'Five Officials' (commentators on the *Wên Hsüan* anthology) rightly take *Shan-kuei* (the title of Song IX) as a synonym for *shan-shên*. The idea that *kuei* were inferior spirits not at all on a par with *shên* is quite late. Mo Tzu (ch. 31) says there are three sorts of *kuei*, those in Heaven (like the former Chou kings), *shên-kuei* of hills and streams, and finally *kuei* who are ghosts of ordinary dead men. In the story of how the Spirit of Mount Hua prophesied the First Emperor's death, in the *Shih Chi* version (6. 27 b) the Spirit is called the *Shan kuei*; while in the *Shui Ching Chu* (19. 5) he is called 'the Lord of Mount Hua.' But like the English word ghost (which once meant 'spirit,' as in the expression Holy Ghost) so too the word *kuei* changed its meaning. To Chu Hsi in the twelfth century *kuei* simply meant ghost, and he consequently assumes that the *shan-kuei* of Song IX is a 'poor creature' (*chien*), not at all on a level with the deities in the other songs.

Song IX, line 15.   That *ling-hsiu* is a term used in speaking to or of deities is clear, but what *-hsiu* means is uncertain. Perhaps something like 'eminent.'

Song IX, line 17.   The Thrice Blossoming is explained as being the *chih-ts'ao*, a plant frequently mentioned, but unidentified. It was often confused with *chih* 'mushroom.'

The Finale.

The title, *Li-hun*, has not been satisfactorily explained. It is conceivable that *hun*, 'soul,' is a mistake for *hun*, 'nightfall,' and that the rites ended at nightfall. In line 1 *hui* in the sense of 'accord' in music is well attested. It occurs, for example, twice in Hsi K'ang's *fu* about the zithern (*Wên Hsüan*, 18), as well as in l. 14 of p. 23 above.

APPENDIX I

The Expansion of Ch'u

Ch'u was a kingdom that in the eighth century B.C. occupied the valleys of the middle Yangtze and Han rivers. In 689 it moved its capital from near Ichang to a point near Kingchow, lower down the Yangtze. In 684 it annexed part of south-eastern Honan and in the next hundred years spread continually northwards and north-eastwards. In 601 Ch'u annexed Shu in western Anhwei. In the sixth century there were setbacks, but in 479 Ch'u annexed Ch'ên, in central eastern Honan. In 333 B.C. the annexation of Wu (southern Kiangsu) made Ch'u an eastern rather than a southern power.

In 278 the Ch'in (western neighbours of Ch'u) captured the Ch'u capital on the Yangtze and Ch'u set up a new capital at Ch'ên in territory annexed (as I have mentioned) in 479. Subsequently the capital was shifted to various points farther east. In 223 B.C. Ch'u became part of the Ch'in empire. After the fall of this empire a descendant of the kings of Ch'u re-established the Ch'u kingdom (208 B.C.), making his capital in eastern Anhwei, and for a time became, nominally at any rate, Emperor of a short-lived Ch'u dynasty. Finally in 202 Ch'u became part of the Han empire.

I have given this brief outline of Ch'u expansion because western scholars, in writing about the Ch'u elegies, have sometimes given the impression that Ch'u was exclusively a southern power.

APPENDIX II

Aoki Masaru's Interpretation of the Nine Songs

The most important modern study of the Songs is, I think, the Japanese scholar Aoki's *Soji Kyūka no Bukyokuteki Kekkō* (The Dramatic Construction of the Nine Songs).* He discusses in detail only Songs V, VI and VII (The Big Lord of Lives, the Little Lord of Lives and the Lord of the East). In these three songs (though not in any of the others) he supposes dialogue between two shamans, one of whom plays the ordinary role of bringing down the deity, while the other acts the part of the deity who descends. He does not support this hypothesis by any ethnological or other parallels; but it certainly fits in quite well with the wording of these songs. On the other hand his view that the Little Lord of Lives was in fact a Little Lady of Lives and attended to the destinies of women in the same way as the Big Lord of Lives attended to those of men seems to me entirely fanciful, and was perhaps not intended to be more than a tentative suggestion.

I have also taken into consideration the principal modern Chinese studies of the Nine Songs, such as those of Wên I-to, Chiang Liang-fu, Ho T'ien-hsing, Wên Huai-sha, Kuo Mo-jo and Yu Kuo-ên.

---

* *Shinagaku* VII (1934). Reprinted in his very interesting volume of essays *Shina Bungaku Geijitsu Kō*.

APPENDIX III

The Commentaries

The earliest commentary on the Nine Songs and the other early literature of Ch'u (that of Wang I, *c.* A.D. 120) is chiefly concerned with the supposed secondary, allegorical meaning. But its author was a man of Ch'u and when he attributes to words an unusual sense he may perhaps be explaining Ch'u dialect words with which he was familiar in his home. His working out of the supposed allegory, as in the instance given above on p. 35, appears sometimes to be very strained and arbitrary. We do not, however, know whether what we possess is the whole of his commentary as he originally wrote it, or merely an abridgment.

The next surviving commentary dates from over a thousand years later. It was by Hung Hsing-tsu (1090–1155), a prolific author and tireless reader who was 'never seen without a book in his hand.' He wrote about the Book of Changes, the Book of History, the *Analects* of Confucius, the chronology of the great prose-writer Han Yü (768–824) and the poems of Tu Fu (713–770). But only his commentary on the collection of Ch'u poetry survives. It was intended as a supplement to the early commentary and not as a new exposition. But it supplies a great deal of information, particularly about the plants, animals, etc., mentioned in Ch'u literature, and also modifies many of Wang I's wilder absurdities.

About fifty years later the famous philosopher Chu Hsi (1130–1200) made a new commentary. It was completed the year before he died, and was almost his last work. His aim, in dealing with the Nine Songs, was to keep the literal meaning and the supposed allegorical meaning separate, which previous commentators had not tried to do. But in explaining the literal meaning he always had the allegory at the back of his mind and where different interpretations are possible he is tied down to choosing one that fits in with his conception of the moral and political allegory. Large parts of his commentary are taken straight from Hung Hsing-tsu without any indication of where they come from. In his preface he merely mentions Hung Hsing-tsu along with Wang I as having been minute in linguistic annotation, but unable to grasp the underlying 'great idea,' which in Chu Hsi's parlance means that they had failed to interpret the poems in terms of Chu Hsi philosophy.

INDEX